Insects that Live in Families

Words by Dean Morris

Raintree Childrens Books
Milwaukee • Toronto • Melbourne • London

Library of Congress Number: 77-8254

1 2 3 4 5 6 7 8 9 0 81 80 79 78 77

Printed and bound in the United States of America.

Library of Congress Cataloging in Publication Data

Morris, Dean.
    Insects that live in families.

    (Read about)
    Includes index.
    SUMMARY: Discusses the behavior of bees, ants, and
other insects that live in colonies.
    1. Insect societies—Juvenile literature.
[1. Insect societies. 2. Insects] I. Title.
QL496.M75 595.7'05'24 77-8254
ISBN 0-8393-0001-8 lib. bdg.

This book has been reviewed
for accuracy by

Carl W. Albrecht
Curator of Natural History
The Ohio Historical Society

Insects that
Live in Families

yellow-jacket
wasp

Some bees and wasps, and all ants and termites live together in families. We say they are "social" insects.

The word *social* means to work together and help each other.

honeybee

Social insects live in nests. The young stay with their parents all their lives.

Each insect has its own job. Social insects work together in much the same way as people do.

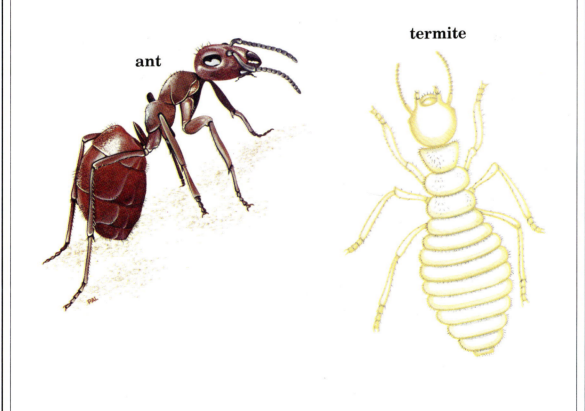

ant

termite

Polistes wasp

The Polistes wasp has a small, thin body.
Like other social insects, it needs a
home that is big enough for a large family.

The queen wasp, or mother, starts the
nest. She chews bits of wood and makes paper.
Then she uses the paper to build little
rooms called cells. The queen lays her
eggs in the cells.

When the young wasps are ready to work,
they build more cells and the queen can
lay more eggs.

The Polistes wasp nest often has a hundred cells.

paper cell

grub

paper cap

egg

stinger

hornet

The hornet is a kind of wasp. Its sting can really hurt. The hornet kills other insects and feeds them to its young. Young hornets are called grubs.

Hornets often build their nests on branches or in hollow trees.

Like the Polistes queen, the hornet queen starts the nest. She lays her eggs in the cells. When the grubs hatch, she feeds them.

When the grubs grow up, the young hornets go out and kill insects on their own. They also help build the nest bigger.

A hornet's nest has hundreds of cells. Paper covers the outside. There is an opening at the bottom.

outside
of nest

inside
of nest

The honeybee's nest is even bigger than the hornet's. It has thousands of cells. Each cell has six sides. The cells, joined together, are called a honeycomb.

worker

queen

drone

Each nest has three kinds of honeybee.

The biggest is the queen bee, or mother. There is only one queen in each nest.

Next in size are the male bees. Males do no work at all. They are called drones.

The worker bees are the smallest. They work very hard in the nest.

honeybee's leg

pollen "basket"

The worker bees find food and bring it to the young bees in the nest. They take sweet nectar from flowers and change it into honey. They also get pollen from flowers. They carry the pollen in bunches of hairs called "baskets" on their back legs.

Honeybees have a good way to tell each other where to find food. When a worker finds a place where flowers are blooming, it flies back to the nest. There it does a dance on the comb. From the direction of the dance and the way the worker wiggles as it dances, the other bees can tell where the flowers are. Bees use the sun to help them find their way.

sun

nest

comb

sun

nest

comb

The cells in a honeycomb are used in different ways, like rooms in a house. Some cells hold honey. Some are filled with pollen. The queen lays eggs in the empty cells. In one day a queen can lay more than a thousand eggs.

The young workers feed the queen and take care of the eggs. After the eggs hatch into small, white grubs, the grubs have to be fed. Grubs that will grow into queens are fed a special food called royal jelly.

When the grubs have had enough food, workers close up their cells with wax. Inside, the grubs slowly grow and change into young bees. They bite their way through the wax covering when they are big enough to leave their cells.

Older workers keep feeding the young bees until they are strong.

small grub

changing grub

young bee

After a while the bee family gets too big for the nest. Then the queen flies off to make a new nest. Many of the workers go with her. A few drones do too. They fly off in a big group called a swarm.

The rest of the workers stay in the old nest. They wait for a new queen to chew her way out of a cell.

A swarm of bees looks like this. When the swarm stops to rest, a few workers go to look for a place to build a new nest. When they find a good place, the queen and all the bees fly off to start the nest.

Some people keep bees to get their honey. If you have ever tasted honey, you know why people like to eat it.

The huts in which people keep bees are called hives. The queen lays her eggs in cells at the bottom of the hive. There are no eggs in the top cells. Worker bees fill them with honey.

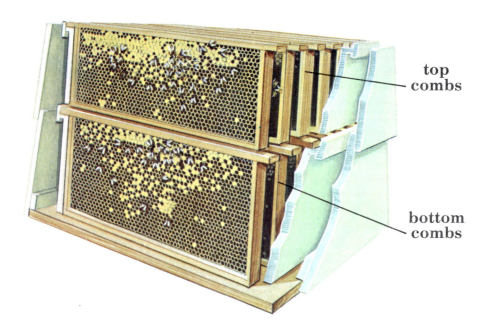

top combs

bottom combs

The beekeeper waits
for the top cells to be
filled with honey.
Then he takes the
honey from the hive.

The beekeeper wears
a special helmet so
the bees cannot sting
his face. He puffs
smoke at the bees. It
makes them too sleepy
to sting.

The beekeeper feeds
the bees sugar and
water in the winter.
There are not enough
flowers to keep the
hive alive in cold
weather.

Families of ants make big nests on the ground. The nests are called anthills. They are made of earth and dead leaves. The nests have many rooms and tunnels inside.

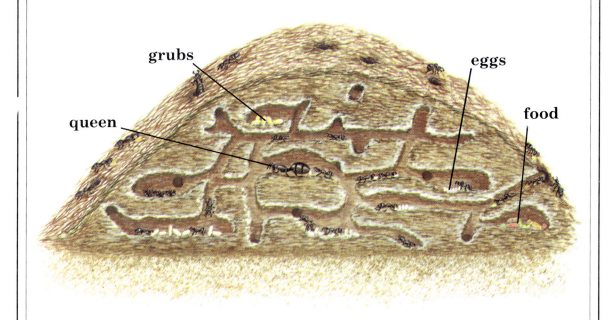

grubs

eggs

queen

food

Thousands of ants live in a nest. There are a few male ants, but they do not work. Most of the ants in the nest are worker ants. The workers are female. The queen ant, like the queen bee, lays all the eggs. When she is young, the queen ant has wings. Before she lays her eggs, the wings fall off. She gets very fat.

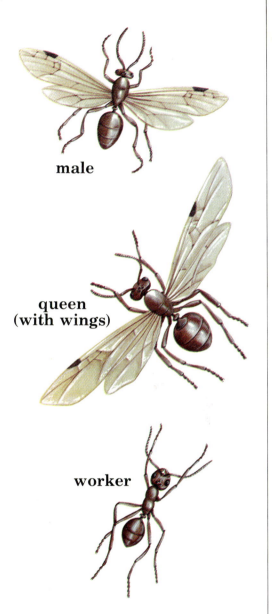

male

**queen
(with wings)**

worker

When the queen lays her eggs, the workers pick them up in their mouths. They carry the eggs to a special room where they will be warm and safe. The workers look after the young ants in the nest too.

If enemies come, the workers run to hide the eggs and protect the young ants. Big guard ants make a circle around the nest. Their job is to fight the enemies.

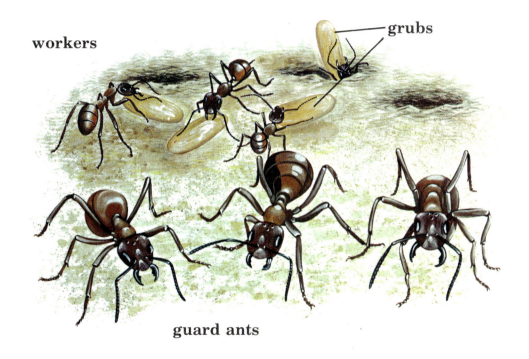

workers

grubs

guard ants

Ants help each other in many ways.
These ants are carrying a leaf back to their
nest. They will use the leaf to fix holes
in the nest. The leaf is much bigger
than they are, but the ants work together.

feelers

Ants can "talk" to each other. They do it by rubbing their feelers together.

When an ant is in danger, it squirts acid at its enemies to scare them away.

These leaf-cutting ants live in the ground. They have strong jaws that cut up leaves. They carry the leaves back to the nest. There other workers chew the leaves into small pieces. Mold grows on the leaves. The ants eat the mold.

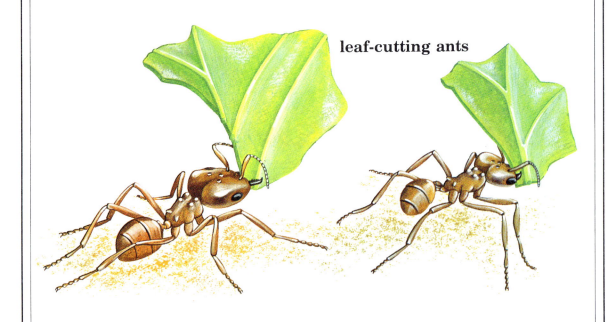

leaf-cutting ants

These ants keep a herd of plant lice called aphids. The aphids make a kind of sweet juice, called honeydew, which ants like. The ants get the juice by rubbing the aphids with their feelers.

Some ants that live in dry places store food. Certain young workers are picked to be "honey pots." Other workers feed them honeydew, and the honey-pot ants hold the food in their bodies. They spend their lives hanging upside down from the top of the nest. When food is scarce, the workers go to the honey-pot ants and eat their fill.

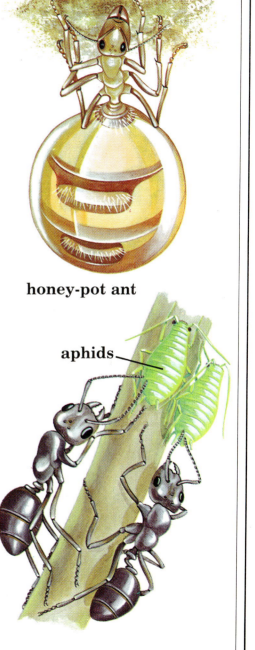

honey-pot ant

aphids

Tailor ants live in Africa. They make
their nests from leaves. The young ants
make silk threads. Worker ants use the
silk to sew the leaves together.

Instead of using needles, the worker ants sew with their mouths. The finished nest is safe and strong.

Army ants do not
build nests. They move
from place to place in
a long line, like
marching soldiers.
As many as 150,000
ants march together.

The ants eat any small animals that get in their way. If a house is in their path, they march through it.

The queen lays her eggs when the army ants stop to rest. Workers carry the eggs and young ants in their mouths.

Army ants move about at night and on cloudy days because bright light kills them.

This is a family of termites. The king and queen live in the middle of the nest. The hind-body of the queen becomes very large as it fills with eggs. She can lay as many as 80,000 eggs in a day!

Workers and soldiers hatch from the eggs. The workers make the nest bigger and feed the young termites. The soldiers protect the nest. They sit with their big jaws and heads pointed away from the queen.

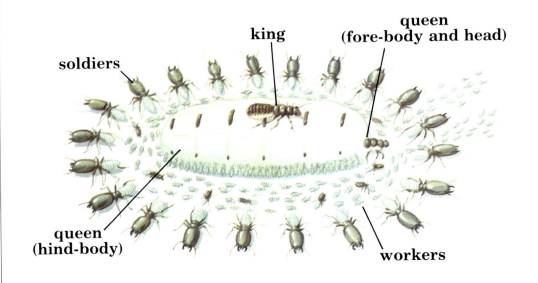

soldiers

king

queen
(fore-body and head)

queen
(hind-body)

workers

Termites in Africa make giant nests from mud. Some of their nests are much bigger than a person. Millions of termites live in these big nests.

Termites eat all kinds of wood—even the walls of houses. Some termites dig into the ground to find water.

hornet

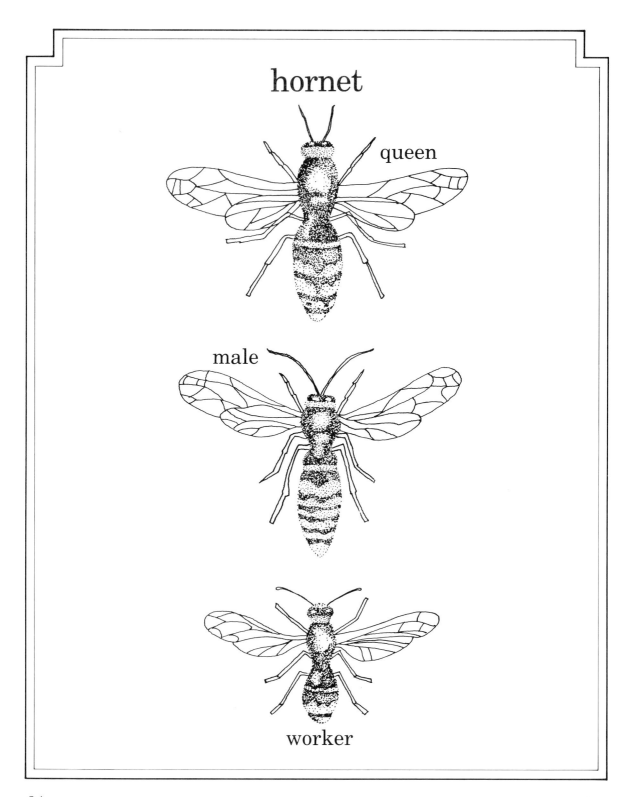

queen

male

worker

wood ant

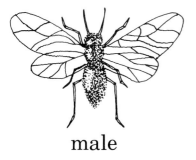

male

worker

queen

termite

queen

king

worker

soldier

wasp

queen

male

worker

honeybee

queen

drone

worker

Where to Read About the Insects that Live in Families

ant (ant) *pp. 4, 5, 20-31*

army ant (är′ mē ant) *pp. 30-31*

bee (bē) *p. 4*

honeybee (hun′ ē bē′) *pp. 4, 10-19*

honey-pot ant (hun′ ē pot′ ant) *p. 27*

hornet (hôr′ nit) *pp. 8-9*

leaf-cutting ant (lēf′ kut′ ing ant)
 p. 26

Polistes wasp (pō li′ stēz′ wosp) *pp. 6-7*

tailor ant (tā′ lər ant) *pp. 28-29*

termite (tur′ mīt) *pp. 4, 5, 32-33*

wasp (wosp) *pp. 4, 6-7*

yellow-jacket wasp (yel′ ō jak′ it
 wosp) *p. 4*

Pronunciation Key for Glossary

a	a as in **cat, bad**
ā	a as in **able,** ai as in **train,** ay as in **play**
ä	a as in **father, car**
e	e as in **bend, yet**
ē	e as in **me,** ee as in **feel,** ea as in **beat,** ie as in **piece,** y as in **heavy**
i	i as in **in, pig**
ī	i as in **ice, time,** ie as in **tie,** y as in **my**
o	o as in **top**
ō	o as in **old,** oa as in **goat,** ow as in **slow,** oe as in **toe**
ô	o as in **cloth,** au as in **caught,** aw as in **paw,** a as in **all**
oo	oo as in **good,** u as in **put**
o͞o	oo as in **tool,** ue as in **blue**
oi	oi as in **oil,** oy as in **toy**
ou	ou as in **out,** ow as in **plow**
u	u as in **up, gun,** o as in **other**
ur	ur as in **fur,** er as in **person,** ir as in **bird,** or as in **work**
yo͞o	u as in **use,** ew as in **few**
ə	a as in **again,** e as in **broken,** i as in **pencil,** o as in **attention,** u as in **surprise**
ch	ch as in **such**
ng	ng as in **sing**
sh	sh as in **shell, wish**
th	th as in **three, bath**
<u>th</u>	th as in **that, together**

GLOSSARY

These words are defined the way they are used in this book.

acid (as′ id) a substance that tastes sour, sharp, or biting

alive (ə līve′) living; not dead; having life

anthill (ant′ hil) a pile of small pieces of dirt, formed when ants dig an underground nest

aphid (ā′ fid *or* af′ id) a small insect that feeds on liquid from plants

beekeeper (bē′ kēp′ ər) a person who takes care of bees and beehives

bloom (bloom) to have flowers

body (bod′ ē) the whole of an animal or plant

bunch (bunch) many things fastened or growing together

cannot (kan′ ot *or* ka not′) is not able; can not

cell (sel) a small space in which a bee lays an egg or keeps honey

chew (cho͞o) to use teeth or jaws to
grind up food

cloudy (klou′ dē) covered over with
clouds

drone (drōn) a male bee, one that does
not do any work

fed (fed) gave a person or animal food
to eat

feeler (fē′ lər) a part of an insect's
body that helps the insect know what it
is touching or smelling

female (fē′ māl) of the sex that has
babies or produces eggs

fix (fiks) to make something work or to
put something together after it breaks

grub (grub) the time of some insects' lives
when they look like worms

guard (gärd) watching over someone or
something; protecting

hatch (hach) to come from inside an egg

helmet (hel′ mit) a head cover that is
used to protect a person from being hurt

herd (hurd) a group of several animals

that are kept together while they are
raised or while they are being moved from
one place to another

hind-body (hīnd′ bod′ ē) the back part of
an insect's body

hive (hīv) a small house or box that
many bees live in together

hollow (hol′ ō) having an empty space
inside

honeycomb (hun′ ē kōm′) many cells, each
with six sides made of wax, made and used
by bees to keep honey in

honeydew (hun′ ē dōō′ *or* dyōō′) a sweet
kind of juice made by aphids

hut (hut) a small building

insect (in′ sekt) a small animal with a
hard outer covering and without a backbone,
such as a fly or ant, and usually with six
legs and two or four wings

jaw (jô) the upper or lower hard mouthpart

jelly (jel′ ē) a soft, clear, firm
substance

juice (jōōs) the liquid from fruits,

vegetables, and meats

leaf (lēf) one of the flat, green parts
that grow from a plant stem

lice see **louse**

louse (lous) a very small insect that
lives by sucking liquid from plants or
blood from animals *plural* **lice**

male (māl) of the sex that can father
young

million (mil′ yən) the number 1,000,000

mold (mōld) a fuzzy growth that forms on
decaying or damp animal or plant material

nectar (nek′ tər) a sweet-tasting liquid
formed inside a flower

next (nekst) after this

pollen (pol′ ən) yellow powder made by a
plant which the plant needs to form seeds

royal (roi′ əl) having to do with, or
belonging to a king or queen

silk (silk) soft, shiny threads made by
some insects

sleepy (slē′ pē) having a hard time
staying awake

social (sō′ shəl) having to do with insects or animals that live in groups together

soldier (sōl′ jər) a person who is part of a group that is trained to fight in battles

squirt (skwurt) to force out liquid in a narrow stream through a small opening

sting (sting) a wound made by an insect

swarm (swôrm) a group of bees all flying together to a place where they will make a new nest

thousand (thou′ zənd) the number 1,000

thread (thred) a long, thin cord spun by a caterpillar to make a cocoon

tunnel (tun′ əl) an underground or underwater passage

upside down (up′sīd doun′) turned so the top part of something is on the bottom

wax (waks) a substance bees make to form the sides of honeycomb cells

wiggle (wig′ əl) to make short movements from side to side

worker (wur′ kər) a female bee, ant, or termite that does most of the work but does not reproduce young insects

Bibliography

Burton, Maurice, and Burton, Robert, editors.
The International Wildlife Encyclopedia.
20 vols. Milwaukee: Purnell Reference
Books, 1970.

FitzGerald, Cathleen. *Let's Find Out About Bees.*
New York: Franklin Watts, 1973.
Describes the busy life in a beehive where
the queen, drone, and worker perform
specific functions as contributing
members of a tightly organized community.

Hutchins, Ross E. *Hop, Skim, and Fly: An Insect
Book.* New York: Parents Magazine Press,
1970.
Describes the life cycle and physical
characteristics of many different kinds
of insects.

Kaufmann, John. *Insect Travelers.*
New York: William Morrow & Company,
1972.
Discusses the travels of insects—how they
time them, where they get the power for
them, and how they navigate.

Kohn, Bernice. *The Busy Honeybee.* New York:
Four Winds Press, 1972.
Describes the characteristics and duties
of the different kinds of bees in a hive
and explains how honey is harvested.

McClung, Robert M. *Bees, Wasps, and Hornets and How They Live.* New York: William Morrow & Company, 1971.
Describes the common characteristics of most membrane-winged insects and explores in further detail the specific characteristics of the different wasps, bees, and hornets belonging to this group.

Pallister, John. *The Insect World.* New York: Home Library Press, 1963.
Some of the most common insects in the central and eastern United States are described. General information about their structure, growth, and relation to man is given.

Shuttlesworth, Dorothy, and Swain, Su Zan Noguchi. *The Story of Ants.* Garden City, N.Y.: Doubleday & Company, 1964.